OPUS # 1 SERIES

JOURNEY WITHOUT END

Henry Gilfond

JOURNEY WITHOUT END

PHILOSOPHICAL LIBRARY
New York

for EDYTHE

JOURNEY WITHOUT END

1

PRELUDE TO JOURNEY

The cradled continents stretch unbroken
between the name and the shadow
and in the dark of morning,
before the curtains of the mist are culled from dreamwept eyes,
I begin this solitary journey.

I bring you a sprig of wildflower,
I bring you the crag of hills and morning,
I bring you the brake flaked sea and the screaming gull.

How deep are the rivers of the forest of the heart?
Who charts their course?

Oh my beloved, my thorn and my flower,
the torment of the moon
sears the wind of my ships
and my child is sucked in your womb.

The infant sleeps in the dream of its father,
caresses the fingers of eternity
with the buds of its mouth,
wakes in the breast of the mother,
fondles the face of heaven
with the suck of its hands.

What mouth has turned within my soils,
what bird has torn my nest,
feed at the fountains of my heart,
feed at the milk and forever,
feed at the stations of all my lamenting voyages.

I speak of my mother—torn in the rocks of mountains,
cave for the river and winds of all the oceans,
hollows in the hills and the sea for the fish that walk in it,
mirrored fruit and the hidden fountains,
alien strain of soundless psalm, stringless instrument,
dancing my feet in the orb of her singing.

I speak of my father—the tall hill on the utmost mountain,
a crag to climb, leaving the flesh and the blood on its tongues,
a tor to mount, dissemble, destroy, eating and loving
each rock on its face, each stream of its heart.

Count, count the fears of my father
and the midnight mass under the spill of stars,
dead moons combed in the moors of their confusion,
count the fears and the fevered tenderness of my mother,
salute and the hot suns sealing the orbits of the womb,
grain rising against the northern lights,
muting shades encasing the forever death,
count the night and the day and the addition of wings
and gills and the scale of the reptile;

from this soil, from this liquid legend,
from concupiscence and the seal of mouth on the lips of death,
I came among you,

shout to the morning, farewell to night,
swell of sea and the cat creeping in the col
     and the cull of the nightdrop,
I came, and I am, and with the strike of skies
and the leaf looming among the sand-drifts,
I will be.

BEGINNING

This is the beginning—the brass prelude and the belly dancers
    in the eastern firmament;
this is the beginning—the drums of hands in the morning
    and the convulsing thunder in the hallways;
this is the beginning—the meeting of the breast and
    the tremor of the constellations,
    incoherent galaxies,
    primal loins in the afternoon,
    the first revelation
    and the evening of its miracle.

      My love has turned her face to the east
      and the sun rises on the song on her mouth;
      sing praise for the shout in her hands,
      for the nesting birds on her fingers,
      for the flowers love-
      locked in the breast of her throat.

This is the beginning—toys of heaven and the cards of the oracles,
    seed and forest, hills and the mountains;
this is the beginning—the grayed gull in the spread sky
    and the sea begging at the sands for all its beaches;
    the cry of the infant at the breast of time
    and the sad music of the albatross;

4

MORNING—GOOD MORNING

The petrel sits at my shoulder
and I sing in the wind.

Good morning!
I say to you good morning
and to the morning good morning.
I say good morning to the stem of the sloe and the leaf
      of the apple in October, to the pomegranate
and to the seedling sucking for root in April's soucient soil.
I say good morning to the grape on the lending vine in the seam
      and dream of autumn's lean and weaning weathers
and to the lotus preening in the summer waters,
to the rill in the hill and the tides singing on all my beaches.
I say good morning to the day and the rain and the wind
      pouring the severing mist across my windows;
and I say good morning to the infant at the breast
      and the saraband among the sycamores;
to the blush of love of the stag
and the rush of love of the turtle
I say good morning and good morning and good morning.

And to you, my love, I say good morning
and to the kiss of the lips on the doorsteps of your mouth
and to the embrace of all our mornings,
of all the madrigals of all our yesterdays
and for all the hosannas of all our tomorrows.

Good morning, good morning, good morning.

We are the playwrights, poets, the makers of words,
inventing the name, the time, the place;
we seek the birth of the infant,
discover death, the resemblance,
the speech, the rain of torment,
as guilt were not enough and we must hear
the anguish of the advocate again, again.

Who reads the blood of our walk?
Who scans the rood of our road?
Who knows for certain the portraits we have painted,
the drunken masses of our confessionals,
the concupiscent love we have sainted?

We are the playwrights, the poets,
we spill in the afternoons of our visitations
the images of our sons
on the blank pages of our poverties,
discovering truth in the shell of an egg,
in the infinite noise of the leaf in a garden,
in the fragile kiss of morning.

Summer bends its wing in the autumn solstice
and April's promise is wind in the hollow.

Who sits in the shadow and dreams of the sun,
the play is begun.

9

ARENA

Let me take you
   where love dies in the afternoon,
where the trumpet issues
   the invitation and death comes
   riding among the assenting populace
   in ribbons and sun
   and the shadow black on its throat,
where the cape is red with promise
   and the echoes of the dream and the drum
   tear fruit from the dust
   and fear moves quickly
   behind the borrowed barriers.

Torments of invention:
   cape of desire
   and the subtle invitation
   to the tryst
   among the lists of sun
   and the darkness against its walls
     (I will meet you, my love,
     at the last gate
     and your eyes will be blind
     in the wheels of my thunder)

and the thrust of the lance,
play of steel
and the horse that spills its love
against the horns of the covenant
   (I wait, my love, against the noise of the sand
   and the sun sweating its face against my haunches)
and the running of spikes
and the blood that meets them
   (and this I ask, my love,
   and this I ask,
   and love meets love in the dark of the hour
   and the shadow meets with the sun)

and the sword,
concealed in the apron of the afternoon,
thrusts its blade
into the opening wound

and love, in the dust of time
and the noise of its departure
on the sterile sands and the shadow of the hour,
splinters the arena of its dream
with the broken drums of its agony,
with the muted trumpets of the afternoon,
with its dying.

   The shroud is on the field
   and death has turned its back on the players;
   and the players, the blood pouring from the soils,
   hold out their hands for pulse of another—
   who, when the land was less rigid, was his brother?

September is on the sands
and the sea without sail.

Rock gently in the arms of tomorrow,
suck sweetly the sibyl crust,
dream with the birds of sorrow,
tomorrow is the grain of dust.

The stables of the sea are cleaned of time
and the sands lie buried in their waters.

10

THE WIND IS FROM THE NORTH

I have wrapped death in the image of my love
and found her a place in September
and the turn of the leaf,
the freight of the wind,
the spill of my heart
is her weeping.

The wind is from the north,
beginning and ending mingle in unpremeditated pact,
the folds of fall rip rudely around our lifted skirts,
concealing the first act.

The audience, the mummied face and the arranged eye,
gesture from the pit, approve, uncertain,
and September's last red summer cry
signs its name to the curtain.

We are the actors; we do not applaud;
divorced by rent of tent,
divided among the masks of our mantled lanterns,
we seek the separate cubicles of our memories,
repeating the phrase of our preludes
(tenebrous phrase, tenebrous prelude)

remembering with the shadow of the leaf
the mirrors of our faces,
the dark of our hands,
morning and afternoon, and the turn of our tables
in the numbers we could not count
on the fingers of our fortunes.

The wind is from the north and God walks the lobbies
        of his tender theatres;
act one is set, the beginning, the names, the place of things;
what comes with winter, spring and sun again
rehearses its worried thunder in the empty caves of the wings.

Rest, rest your dreams in the fold of my arms.
There beginning and ending, in brief compassion,
mend the wounds of time and soughly fashion
never, forever,
in the arrow of the bird
come to sing
among the muted nightingales
and the willows in your hair.

Our hands touch the doorsteps of the afternoon,
memory files its face among our liturgies.
We forget the contemplation of the journey
in the dream and the pities.

11

IF IN LATE OCTOBER

If in late October
a burst of sun should split your window
and a remnant leaf fall from the wind,
if in the scrannel clamor of the lonely season
a reach of sky should comb your hair
and birds come to sit upon your fingers,
if in the swell of autumn's peacock choir
a hand of August touch your hand
and sough of summer kiss your mouth,
how will you know if God or children
work at miracles
and who intrudes upon the sill
and who invades the heart?

Kiss, kiss with your mouth the pennies I have found you,
embrace the trace of my mouth;
steel and water melt the day of grief
and my boats find beach
in the memory.

These things of heart and mind I must remember
before I turn the veil for dark November.

12

EVENING

The skies are lulled with love of summer's skein
before the evening draws its blind
and the last lean shadow claims the darkness
in cold November's wind.

(After the lilac and the summer rose,
the crocus and the winter snows.)

We walk at the edge of sun
and look among the distant gulls
for fading light;
we turn our backs
at the edge of mountains
and look on night.

How like a dream was this day between us,
blending the rise and the fall of the sun
with shadows of all our memories.

Blessed are those with pain to remember
and the ache of the lost keep,
blessed are those who weep
among the ashes of forgetting.

How like my love is this night between us,
mending the lean and the full of the moon
with memories of shadow.

   Blessed are those who walk on the waters
      of their visitations,
   blessed who salve their worried wounds
      with the mirrors of their blessed agonies.

How do we destroy what day has done
in the shallow casements of the evening's sun?

         We have lost the way
         in sun of day.
         How shall we find haven
         when night and love
         are with the raven?

13

WINTER

In the evening of our calendars
we waited in the waning line of time,
in the calendars of evening
purchased with the fear of our fingers,
in the closed arenas of our departures,
the vacant seats of our voyages.

    Who sits with me and looks for God across the proscenium?
    Who sits with me, dissembling
    memory and desire in the plays of yesterday?
    Who sits with me in the darkness of ourselves, trembling?

Wrapped in the jackets of our councils,
wrapped in the coats of our concealment,
we discover our mouths in the face of the mask,
our throats in the cry of the curtain,
applaud, uncertain,
the shadows we have paid for and lost,
the images we have seen and lost,
the mirrors we have made and lost;

    and in this melancholy moment
    retrieve the bird

and move our sacks to other seas, other valleys,
the labels of our journeys
sewn in the coats of our betrayals.

How shall we know where we go,
or where we have been?

How shall we greet the reasoning of our books,
sleep the fears we have worn,
the courage we have borrowed?

Disrobe the armors of uncertain logic,
catch at whispers,
cry, "Forever and the firmament!"

We will hear you even in the closets of our bones,
in the manufactured pities of our minds,
in the fevers of the wind and the skies rattling
        our parapets,
tremble
before all the fires we have stoked in all the houses
        of our battlements,
and suffer
in the darkness of the tendered hour
all the feeble choirs
of all our rampant
and undiminished
trepidations.

Winter is the evening of the voyage,
the end of season;
the earth opens its bosom for the wanderer
and closes its doors on all his voyages.

14

$4+4=8$

Lean against the half of the moon
lifting the windows of the night,
read the signs on the corpse and the highway
leeching the glass of its light.

$4+4=8$
St. Peter waits us at the gate.

Night drops its shade about our feet
and we are naked in its mirrors.

We thank thee, Lord, for our daily bread,
for the harp of hair, when we are dead.

Now are the streets of my heart empty
and death directs the traffic.

Covet not your neighbor's wife,
if you would seek the after-life.

Wheel the hoop of the three-ringed midget,
parade on the pachyderm's back;
fear is the flower of evening
and the flower is black.

The Lord is my shepherd. He grooves the grave
to hold these bones I cannot save.

Fix your teeth on the bearded lady,
retrieve the ball for the seal,
the meek inherit
the Virginia Reel.

Dance with the Lord and the memory of his covenants,
sing with the opulent fears in the breast
of his tabernacles,
I dance with the breast of my love
and sing with her lips on my fingers.
Evening black or sunned with moon,
I plant my feet on the bed of its throat
and press my mouth on her heart.

My Lord, do I deceive you?

What piece of bookkeeping do you write
against the billboard signs,
advertising the small fright?
The affluent display
of desperate illusion
in the maze of day
darkens in the evenings of our dissolution.

Shake the hand of the corpse.
Say farewell to the flutter of the grass
and the flight of the madrigal.
There, at the corner of the star,

between oblivion and tomorrow,
she waits for you on the chorus of the heart,
dancing the lips of her flimsy,
whistling the wind of her whipple,
and the fool in the streets
that yesterday were swept and scoured
makes a poetry of the wound
and the arrow.

Lord, do I deceive you?

How strange that we arrange
the circumstances to fit our clothes.

Who looks for peace
among the warring factions of the heart?
Who sits among the winters of the voyage
and looks for April in its snows?

The leaves of my mouth are with the wind,
the frost of my throat with the moon;
my anguish
spills against the treason.

Do I grieve you, Lord?

I will not pretend to welcome the end of my turbulent days,
nor will I contend when nights descend upon my stay
that I defend too well my post with arms,
nor cry alarms.

As time is measured by the course of sun,
my labors finished or undone,
what death to man has meant,
I am lost to meet its argument.

I shall go, I know, whether I will it or no,
and find less pain, if less I find,
that where I lie, there others lay
in stone, in soil, perhaps in mind.

And yet, do not mistake this reverie
for resignation.
Better think it
another assignation.

For love is not consigned
to time of day, and I would find
at the depot of my journey
love's attorney
to sue the dust or clay or sea
for love's own poetry.

And this were not too much to ask
since, loving love so much as I,
if death be loveless,
I will not die.

Do I grieve you, Lord?

    Lean against the half of the moon,
    read the corpse on the moat;
    I dance with the feet of my beloved
    and her song is on my throat.

15

SLEEP AND DREAM

Sleep moves its easy hands on the lids of your fevers
and you lie, at last, your lips with love.

   With whom do you walk now,
   in which wash of wave,
   what well of willing wandering waters?
   How far have you ferried,
   what found on fringe and ferruled furnitures
   of all your furrowed flight?

I am lately concerned with the distortions of the sun,
with the waking of moons in the sleep of my dreams;
that which in the morning clogs the windows of my coat,
in the evening unravels my seams.

   God mounts the sill of my tongue
   and the idiot dances to the reed.
   Who addresses the night of the forest?
   Who sings to the weed?

I am lately concerned with myself and another,
sound and torment,

and I am both,
both sound and torment,
instrument and the player of music.

And I am confirmed in the sanity of the naked word
and reason, and I wing my throat,
skirt falling bird
and treason.

I am lately concerned.

THE WHITE HORSE

The white horse is on the street again,
ruffles its ears to the bell on the clock,
and the thief puts his torso
on the wheel of a tree,
asking the concupiscent clamor of indifference.

The yellowed mule is in the corn,
eating its belly in the eclipse of the moon,
and the hangman
slips the feathered noose
about the neck of the cock
crowing its crock
in the morning chronicle.

The white seagull roosts on the utmost flag in coventry,
creaking its white delight in the blackest quarter of the night
and the indifferent eagle, from the utmost sanctuaries
        of its white mountains,
swoops down on the gull
to eat it up.

  I ride the white horse
      through the daffodil that grows
      in the disused argument of its waters.

I ride it through the wheel and the unsubtle
   insistence of its ringing bell.
I turn the mule upon its haunches
   and scream its belly to the eastern winds,
   the impatient gull losing its seed
   in the ditch of its fumbling persuasion.

I loosen the arms of the tree
   and right its feet for the unwilling pavement.
I lose the hangman and his noose
   and screw the crock of neck
   that crows the morning
   before the glory of the morning
   announces sun.

   The ship drowns at sea
   and all hands are lost
   and the list of passengers
   floats its hat upon the waters.

   I investigate the disaster and discover:
   bubble of oil
   and a card marked:
   address me at the intersection of the table.

   Whom shall I address?
   at which table?

   All is calculation, all in time,
   and the multiplication measures the zero,
   where the ship foundered
   and deserted its dominion.

The choir boy, in full dress white collar,
dives into the river,
doesn't come up.

He is looking for a souvenir for the mother of God.
It will be a long time before he remembers.

The choir boy has found the sea-wormed cask of a rotted barge,
rests his head with a segment of seagull's bones.

We will send the men of the press to interview him,
and a photographer to bring up his picture.

How do you play your saxaphone?
Where is the best place to eat?
Who does your laundry?
Where do you sleep?

No comment.
No comment.
No comment.
No comment.

No one knows how long it has run
nor when there will be a change in program.
The cast repeats itself,
and I wait in line,
the price of admission enmeshed in the vestibules of time;
there is no standing room for this performance.

Night ends in the street first,
moving its monuments on the ass of the moon;
in the converted stable and its row of stalls,
the curtain comes down abruptly
and the actors sit on the proscenium
to eat of the darkness.

It is too late for weeping
and the audience does not applaud;
its hands
are washed in the willows.

    The white horse is on the streets again
    and my heart beats
    one two one two.

17

SOMEWHERE I LIVE

Between the darkness of understanding
and the light that turns a crumbling roof to dance

not always—but when
the pavements of the sea sit on my feet
and I carry the unused portions of undecided recipe
in my back pocket.
I would like to smoke my pipe
but the sign says:
THE GENTLEMAN IN THE AISLE IS WANTED IN THE FRONT OFFICE.

I am not the gentleman in the aisle
and I am not wanted in the front office
but I go.
I walk on the edge of all the benches
and the pigeons follow me.
"Poor pigeons," I think but do not say,
"I have no meat in my vest,
and you will find the office closed."
But they follow me and I say,
"There is no sign on the office which reads:
CLOSED FOR THE REMAINDER."

What remainder and how closed?
There is no door here, no window,
no letter box, no lock—
but the remainder is plain.
This I knew before I came to live here.

In the groves of our sleep
the mind stirs to untranquil memory
and we move the obscured carts of our camps
from sickle point to sickle pass.

(The pigeons hobble in the poverty of their parks,
grow fat on the crumbled dreams of my city.)

Do you think I shall count the pages of my calendar torn
and mourn the journey in the strange corn?

What the arrow plants
the wound grows;
sleep moves its easy hands among your fevers
and love
lies the lion
on your breast.

After a while, after the millennium among seas and trees,
you reach for the substance of your mortars and touch
your pillow.

The pillow is wet where your lips have kissed it
and you think:

what did I see in my journey?
whom did I meet?
who wore the frock and turned a wall against a valley?
whose window fell upon a church and blossomed?

You think: this I must remember
and this I must remember, and turn the pillow
and sleep again
and sleep again.

18

WITHOUT END

I have come home
and someone has been here before me,
rearranged my books, my pictures,
the souvenir from the river—
last week's flowers are dried in their beds.

Who answered the bell?
I have forgotten.
Did I turn the key? Did I turn the lock?
That I have forgotten, too.

I know that I have been on a voyage.
(My feet are caked with crocus,
my hands with weed.)
Did I see the widow watering the remains of her children?
Did I see the deer embrace?
Was the mirror I bought second-hand?

Vaguely I recollect the mist I assumed,
the image of the dog walking the speech of the moon at noon.
I went to the theatre often and applauded the actors,
then drank coffee
to sober my dismay.

What do they say
who love the images they make?
This is beauty, this is truth.

I count my fingers: ten.
How brilliant we were at the dinner table.

I do not wish to say there is nothing.
Somewhere in my journey I touched upon a lip
and slept with seven years
and the moss
and the aster.

But the journey—
the beginning, the prelude to promise
(if I were sure—
and this I saw—was it among the gulls
gathering for the remains, the boy and the lost canticle?)

    (I would hold you against the wave of the sea
    and kiss the salt on your lips.)

Pity—that I remember, too,
and grief—

  and the rose that wound its thorns
  in the mouth of the wound.

    (This picture I would save—
    I was three then
    and my hair the color of the April sun you brought me.)

Somewhere my father is lost;
    I cannot hear him.
My mother beats the glass of my heart
    one two one two.

And my mirror is the same
except that I detect the signs of the voyage
and this I regret,
as I regret your growing old,
my growing old,
and the end of a chapter,

    except, as the wind turns east
    and the rains come,
    I wet my face in tomorrow's daffodils
    and think:

    How can we think in sun,
    in rain,
    in green, in dark,
    that fall or spring or season
    turn face of love from singing lark
    to death and reason?

The journey does not end

and in the morning
I will play my tambourine
and sing a love song
before breakfast:

    How beautiful is the rain
    melting the sleep from your face.

How beautiful your face
in the nest of your hair.

No end. No end.
Only beginning, beginnings.

Sing with me
or lie with me,
the pigeons of the sun
spill their messengers among your cups
and I would kiss the milk of your lips
and I would kiss the mouth you press
against all the walls of all my remembering.

I found you on the shaft of my heart
and I would keep your fingers there.

What daffodils of music
grow from the drums
of my tambourine.

Only beginning, beginnings,
and the sun sitting on the shadow of the hawk
and the gentle fall of the lamb in the evening.

What is gone we cannot retrieve
but with your heart and mine
I collect the pictures of my design
and turn my face to what the days conceive
for other seas, for other lands,
for the kiss of my fingers and the love of my hands.

The dream is on my sleeve
and the birds pick at it, and sing—
and I kiss each mouth,
each fragment wing,
unraveling the weave.

From where I began this solitary journey,
what heart I spent,
love winds its emblems about my shoulders
and the journey does not end.